GROW YOUR MIND

BUILD RESILIENCE

Written by Alice Harman

Illustrated by David Broadbent

CRABTREE
PUBLISHING COMPANY
WWW.CRABTREEBOOKS.COM

CRABTREE
PUBLISHING COMPANY
WWW.CRABTREEBOOKS.COM

Author: Alice Harman
Series designer: David Broadbent
Illustrator: David Broadbent
Editor: Crystal Sikkens
Proofreader: Melissa Boyce
Print coordinator: Katherine Berti

A trusted adult is a person (over 18 years old) in a child's life who makes them feel safe, comfortable, and supported. It might be a parent, teacher, family friend, social worker, or another adult.

Library and Archives Canada Cataloguing in Publication

Title: Build resilience / written by Alice Harman ; illustrated by
  David Broadbent.
Names: Harman, Alice, author. | Broadbent, David, 1977- illustrator.
Description: Series statement: Grow your mind | Includes index. |
  First published in Great Britain in 2020 by the Watts Publishing Group.
Identifiers: Canadiana (print) 20200219553 |
  Canadiana (ebook) 20200219774 |
  ISBN 9780778781677 (hardcover) |
  ISBN 9780778781752 (softcover) |
  ISBN 9781427125934 (HTML)
Subjects: LCSH: Resilience (Personality trait) in children—Juvenile
  literature. | LCSH: Resilience (Personality trait)—Juvenile literature.
Classification: LCC BF723.R46 H37 2021 | DDC j155.4/1824—dc23

Library of Congress Cataloging-in-Publication Data

Names: Harman, Alice, author. | Broadbent, David, 1977- illustrator.
Title: Build resilience / written by Alice Harman ; illustrated by David
  Broadbent.
Description: New York : Crabtree Publishing Company, 2021. | Series:
  Grow your mind | Includes index.
Identifiers: LCCN 2020015526 (print) |
  LCCN 2020015527 (ebook) |
  ISBN 9780778781677 (hardcover) |
  ISBN 9780778781752 (paperback) |
  ISBN 9781427125934 (ebook)
Subjects: LCSH: Resilience (Personality trait) in children--Juvenile literature.
  | Self-actualization (Psychology)--Juvenile literature.
Classification: LCC BF723.R46 H37 2021 (print) | LCC BF723.R46 (ebook)
  | DDC 155.4/1824--dc23
LC record available at https://lccn.loc.gov/2020015526
LC ebook record available at https://lccn.loc.gov/2020015527

Crabtree Publishing Company

www.crabtreebooks.com   1-800-387-7650
Published by Crabtree Publishing Company in 2021

Published in Canada
Crabtree Publishing
616 Welland Ave.
St. Catharines, Ontario
L2M 5V6

Published in the United States
Crabtree Publishing
347 Fifth Ave.
Suite 1402-145
New York, NY 10116

Printed in the U.S.A./082020/CG20200601

First published in Great Britain in 2020 by The Watts Publishing
Group Copyright © The Watts Publishing Group 2020

CONTENTS

A resilient mindset

Sometimes in life, things don't go exactly the way we want them to. We can find ourselves having to deal with all kinds of frustrating, difficult, or sad situations. We might be struggling to understand a new lesson in class or worrying about someone in our family being sick.

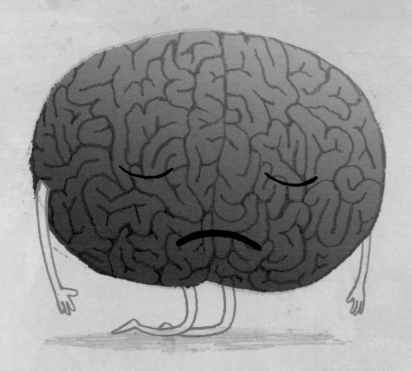

When things get tough, it can feel like we're stuck in that situation forever— like we'll never feel better and there's nothing we can do about it.

But, thankfully, this isn't how things have to be. You can't stop bad things from happening to you, but you can learn to build **resilience**.

This means learning how to keep going and stay positive when things are really challenging. It also means helping yourself recover more quickly from difficulties.

We often think of our brains as being fixed the way they are. This way of thinking is known as a **fixed mindset**. In reality, our brains are always growing and changing. When we think of our brains this way, we are using a **growth mindset**.

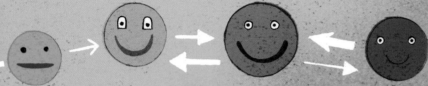

Every person's brain has billions of **neurons**, which pass messages to each other along paths. Our thoughts and actions can help build new paths and strengthen ones that already exist.

This means that your brain can rise to new challenges—even ones that are hard to deal with—and learn and grow from them.

When we're resilient, we keep going even when things get difficult. This is called **persevering**. Although we may struggle during tough times, with some effort we can bounce back and find future success and happiness.

The power of "yet"

Have you ever tried to do something, but couldn't, and thought, "Argh, I just can't do it!"? How does it make you feel? Not great, right?

"I can't do it" can make us feel stuck, like things can't change so there's no point in even trying. But that's not true! Our brains are always changing and growing, and we are able to learn all kinds of new things. So instead of thinking "I can't do it," try switching to "I can't do it YET."

Adding "yet" to a negative statement unlocks a door to a positive future, and encourages us to push it open. It builds our resilience by helping us understand that difficult situations can change and get better.

Write down something that makes you think "I can't do that." It could be anything, from reading a difficult book to talking to a group of friends after a big argument.

Put it into a negative sentence—for example, "I can't read this book." How does it make you feel? Pretty bad, right?

Now add the "yet"—"I can't read this book YET." How do you feel now?

Believing that something could be possible in the future encourages us to think, "So how can I make it happen?" Come up with three "I can" sentences to answer this question, such as "I can practice reading with my parents in the evening."

Effort thermometer

It can be hard to stay resilient if we focus on the outcomes and achievements in our lives, rather than the efforts we've made. We might be disappointed and feel bad about ourselves, even if the negative outcomes are partly or entirely because of things we can't control.

It can help to change our measure of success if we focus on our behavior—which we can control, even if things are difficult and not working out the way we hoped. This way, we can still feel happy and proud of ourselves.

This approach makes us more resilient by encouraging us to keep going through difficult times. We learn that what matters is how we act rather than what the outcome is.

Create an "effort thermometer" to track how much effort you've put into different challenges, such as working through your fears and worries or getting along better with your brother or sister.

You can use the example thermometer on this page to get started. Choose the section of the thermometer with the words and phrases that best describe how much effort you're making.

Remember, your effort score is personal to you. It depends on your mood, how you feel about the task, and so on.

Keep an effort journal of your tasks, scores, and what you learned. You should find that putting in more effort really does help you feel better and learn positive lessons, even if you can't yet see any difference in terms of outcomes.

4

Challenging myself

I find this very difficult, but I'm trying my hardest.

3

Concentrating

I'm trying to meet challenges set by others (teachers/family).

2

Improving

I'm behaving most of the time.

1

Giving up

I'm misbehaving instead of working.

Digging deeper

Have you ever felt so frustrated with how long it's taking to do or learn something that you want to just give up?

From making new friends to learning a new skill, it can be really difficult when things take a while, especially when they are important to us.

So how can we build our resilience to cope with these feelings of frustration? We need to stop worrying about doing things quickly. Instead, we need to see all the positives in giving ourselves time to dig deeper and make lasting change.

When we give things our full, unrushed attention, we may end up understanding them—and ourselves—much better.

Olivia

I used to have a best friend at my school,
and we had so much fun together that I didn't really
care about not spending time with anyone else.

But then he had to move away. Although we could still video call
each other in the evenings, everything changed. I was suddenly
on my own at school and I felt really lonely.

I knew a few people that I talked to a little, but it wasn't the same.
It was awkward trying to get to know them better. I just wanted
to fast-forward to us being close friends.

I talked to my mom and she told me that making good friends was like
building a house. You can build quickly on the surface, but the house
is much stronger if you dig deep foundations for it.

She helped me be patient and keep trying, rather than giving up
and staying lonely. I've become much closer to two friends.
Our friendships feel real now, rather than forced.

Halfway there

A great way to build your resilience is to think about how everything you do helps develop your brain over time (see pages 4–5). You don't have to worry about making mistakes, or not doing things "perfectly," because your efforts are still helping you along your lifelong journey.

Think about it this way—when you start a new, challenging lesson in math, are you starting completely from the beginning?

No! Because earlier in your life you made the effort to learn what numbers are, how to add them together, and other things that are helpful now. We call this your "prior learning."

Try out this activity to discover how your prior learning helps you reach your goals.

1. Draw a line of five squares, with a star in the middle square. Think about the challenge you're facing and write your goal in the final square of the grid.

2. In the squares before the starred middle one, write in the knowledge and skills that you've already worked hard to gain.

3. In the square after the starred middle one, write what you need to do to reach your goal. You can ask an adult to help with this.

4. See, you're already halfway there! And look at how the effort you've put in so far is paying off now.

| Learned to write | Wrote my own poem | ⭐ | Write my own short story | Write a book! |

Try to fail

Everyone makes mistakes, but we may see them as failures. It can make us feel bad when we don't do something perfectly, and we may not want to try again.

In reality, learning from mistakes is a great way to give your brain a big growing boost! You can build your resilience by changing the way you think about mistakes—seeing them as opportunities to grow and learn, rather than failures.

Imagine dropping two balls on the ground—one is inflated, the other is deflated. The deflated one can't bounce back up, but the inflated one can. If we see mistakes as failures, we feel down and deflated when we make them. But if we see mistakes as learning opportunities, it helps us to bounce back up and try again!

Victoria

I was at a big family party a while ago,
and I was showing off a bit in front of my older cousins
because I wanted them to think I was grown-up like them.

I tried to use some of the bigger words we'd learned in class
recently, but they were confused and laughed because what I said
didn't make sense. I guess I got the meanings mixed up.

I felt so silly and embarrassed that I ran off to find my grandma.
I didn't want to go back out and see everyone.

When I told my grandma what had happened, she said she was really
proud that I was trying to challenge myself, and with a bit of practice
I'd have so many more interesting words to use to express myself.

I went back out to the party and joked around with my cousins.
They didn't care at all about my mistake, in fact, they were
worried they'd upset me. I learned how brave I can be, and
realized people don't expect me to be perfect!

POSITIVE PRACTICE

Sometimes, as hard as we try not to, we can feel disappointed or frustrated when things don't go our way.

One thing that can really help build our resilience for these moments is "collecting" positive thoughts. When things get tough, and it feels like nothing is going right, we will have some positive examples to show us this isn't true.

By making an everyday habit of thinking about things to be grateful for or feel good about, you can help your brain bring them to mind much more quickly and easily in difficult times. This can give you a resilience boost to keep on thinking positively.

Try this

Every day, at a time when you're
together with some or all of your family,
have each person take a turn sharing the
following positive experiences from their day:

1. One thing I did today that made someone else happy.

2. One thing that someone else did that made me happy.

3. One thing that I learned.

Later, write down some examples that make you believe
things can change for the better. Next time you feel
down, have a look at this list for some
positive inspiration.

Stronger together

Although developing your resilience can be really helpful and positive, remember that no one expects you to always be happy or deal with everything all by yourself.

It's okay to be upset. Your trusted adults want to know if you are struggling with something so they can listen and help. If anyone or anything is making you feel bad or worried, don't try to deal with it alone. Always talk to a trusted adult.

It can often help you feel better just to share the problem. Other people may have great ideas that will help—ones that you might not have even thought of!

18

Hussein

I found it really hard when we moved to another city last year for my mom's new job. We moved in the middle of the school year so I had to catch up on the work we were doing in my new class. I felt lost, and started worrying so much that I didn't really listen when the teacher was talking.

I didn't want to bother my mom, since she was so busy with her new job and getting us settled in our house. She told me how proud she was of me for doing so well, and I didn't want to disappoint or worry her.

But one day, I had a bad stomachache from worrying, and I told my mom I didn't want to go to school.

We talked over everything and she wasn't disappointed at all. She just wanted to help me, and was glad I told her about my problems. She talked to my teacher. Now we discuss my work and worries every day after dinner.

CHANGE FOR GOOD

When we're struggling with tough
situations, an important part of being
resilient is understanding that things can,
and will, change for the better.

Even if you're in a situation that you can't control,
such as having to leave your friends behind when you
move, there are all kinds of ways things can get better.
You can meet new people and discover new things that
you enjoy. You can also develop new ways of staying close
to your old friends, such as sending each other videos.

We often feel nervous about change and
would prefer things to just stay the same.
It can be really helpful to get used to thinking
about change as something positive.

SOLD

Try out these activities to practice seeing change as a normal and positive part of life. You might think of some of your own activities too—that's even better!

1. Try one new thing a week—whether it's a food, an activity, or listening to a song you've never heard before. Keep a journal of all the new things you've tried, and record what each experience was like. You might find some new favorites!

2. Let go of things you don't need any more. This could be old clothes that don't fit, or books and toys that you've grown out of. Ask an adult to help you recycle them, donate them, or pass them on to someone who can use them.

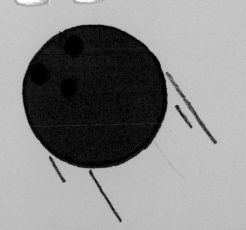

3. Think of something that you didn't really like when you first tried it, and give it another try! It could be an activity or a kind of food. We are always changing, so you might find that you have grown to like it.

SEEING THE FUTURE

Don't worry, you won't need a crystal ball for this, just your imagination!

A great way of building resilience to deal with problems in the present is to learn how to visualize, or create a picture in your mind, of a positive future.

Visualizing a future version of yourself overcoming your problems helps your brain realize that it is possible to do so.

When you feel really stuck or down, it can be hard for your brain to imagine that things can get better. But if you practice this visualization skill regularly, it should be easier to do when you need it most.

Toby

When my uncle died suddenly, it felt like
it left a big hole in my life. He was so funny and kind.
I missed him so much that it actually gave me a pain in
my chest and stomach. I felt like I hadn't had a chance to
say goodbye and I was afraid I'd never feel better about that.

My mom was sad too, and she told me to try something that
was helping her a lot, called "visualization." I imagined a picture of
myself in the future, smiling with my mom as we talked about all
the good times we had with my uncle.

Visualizing that future makes it seem more possible for
me. Instead of feeling so stuck and scared, now I feel like
I've got something positive to work toward.

I talk through my feelings regularly with
my mom and other trusted adults, and I
know it's okay to be sad and take time
to move forward.

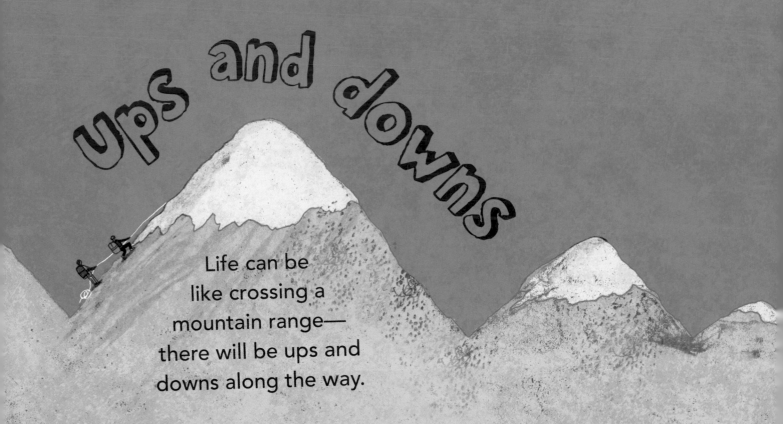

ups and downs

Life can be like crossing a mountain range— there will be ups and downs along the way.

When we're feeling good and things are going well, it might feel like we're at the peak of a mountain. But when events in our life knock us off course, we may feel like we're sliding back down the other side.

If something really serious happens, such as our parents splitting up or somebody we love dying, it might feel like we've slid down so far that we can't climb back up again. This is why it's so important to build resilience so we keep on trying.

Think of your resilience as your brain's climbing kit. Every time you practice building resilience it's like you are adding a bottle of water, a snack, a rope, or some boots to your kit. It all helps make it that much easier to climb back up the mountainside.

Kieran

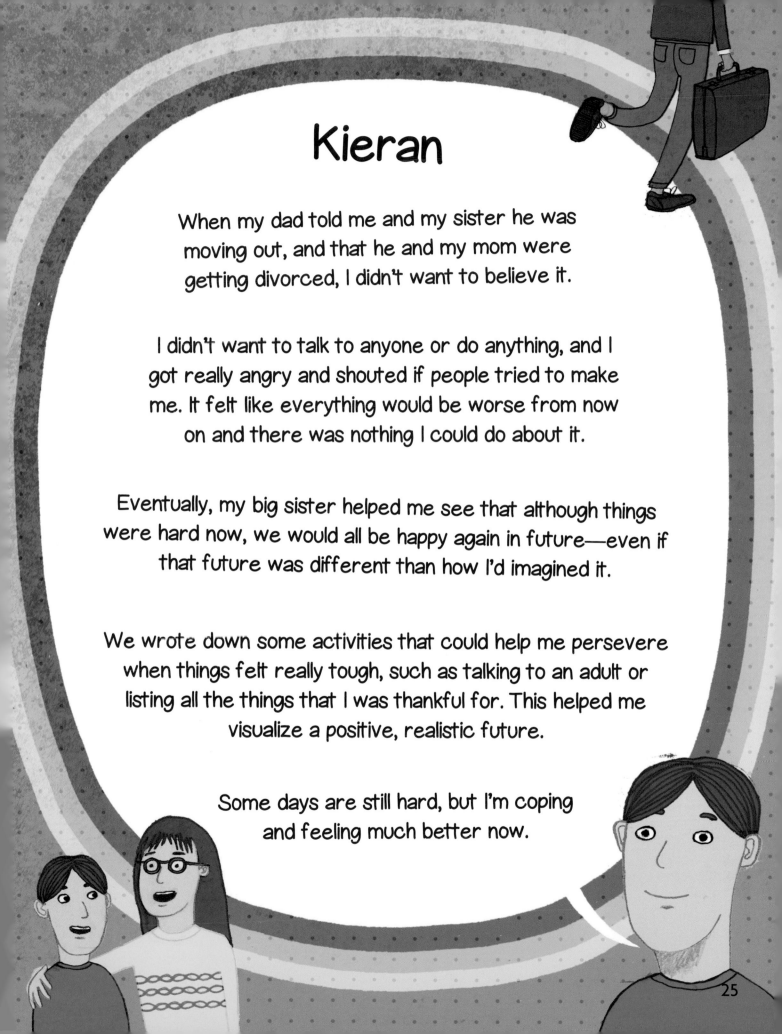

When my dad told me and my sister he was moving out, and that he and my mom were getting divorced, I didn't want to believe it.

I didn't want to talk to anyone or do anything, and I got really angry and shouted if people tried to make me. It felt like everything would be worse from now on and there was nothing I could do about it.

Eventually, my big sister helped me see that although things were hard now, we would all be happy again in future—even if that future was different than how I'd imagined it.

We wrote down some activities that could help me persevere when things felt really tough, such as talking to an adult or listing all the things that I was thankful for. This helped me visualize a positive, realistic future.

Some days are still hard, but I'm coping and feeling much better now.

REST AND RECOVER

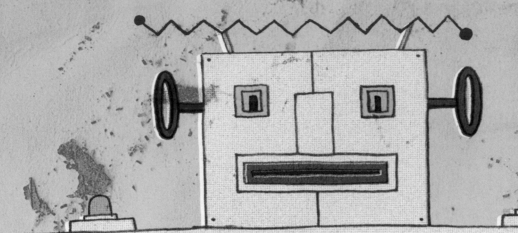

It's important to remember that you're not a machine! It takes effort to use your resilience to face challenges, whether it's new, big ones, or just lots of little ones throughout the day.

We all need time to rest and recover from this hard work. We can't keep going forever without having a break. Working nonstop can make us feel worn out and frustrated, causing our brains to not function well.

This may weaken our resilience to cope when things aren't going exactly as we'd hoped, making us more likely to think "I can't do it!" and give up altogether.

While you take a break, your brain might keep working on challenges for you anyway. Scientists have found that when we relax and stop consciously thinking about a problem, our brains carry on busily making connections between neurons on an **unconscious** level. Thanks, brain!

So what are your favorite ways to give your brain a nice break?

Try to think of five things that make you feel really calm, or that are easy and fun to do. It could be coloring, dancing to your favorite song, playing outside, making up a story, watching cartoons—anything you like!

Make a small "Brain Break" reminder card. Write or draw your five ideas on this card and keep it in your pocket or backpack. When you're feeling worn out or frustrated, take out the card and try out one or more of the ideas.

Get creative

Sometimes if we're facing challenges in life and feel like nothing we try is working, it can be tempting to give up. A great way to build resilience is to learn how to think a little differently.

Looking at the world in creative ways can help unlock and wake up your brain, building pathways and sending neurons jumping into action.

You can practice your creative-thinking skills through all kinds of fun activities, including drawing, making up stories, inventing games, and trying to solve riddles.

By helping your brain open up to more possibilities, you should find it easier to think creatively when you face problems that you're not sure how to solve.

Try out these activities to spark your brain's creative power—or, even better, make up your own!

1. Pick three objects you can see around you and make up a story that includes all of them.

2. Draw three circles, then turn them into anything you want, such as a face, an animal, or maybe a spaceship!

3. Put on your inventor hat and think of three ways to make your favorite game or toy even more fun.

4. Think up some silly "Would You Rather?" questions. For example, would you rather have spaghetti for hair or forks for fingers?

KEEP BUILDING RESILIENCE!

Read through these tips for a quick reminder of how best to build resilience!

Instead of thinking "I can't do that," try switching to "I can't do that YET."

Focus on the efforts you're making, rather than on their outcomes.

Aim to slow down and dig deeper
rather than racing ahead.

Use your previous life experience
to face new challenges.

See mistakes as
opportunities to
learn and grow.

Make it an everyday habit to share positive experiences with your family.

Talk to a trusted adult if you feel upset or worried.
Don't try to deal with it all by yourself.

Try new experiences and challenge your old, set ideas.

Visualize a positive future to help your brain imagine it being possible.

Keep on building your resilience even when things are
going well, to help you learn how to deal with tougher times.

Discover what calms you down when
you feel worn out and frustrated.

Practice your creative thinking and problem solving in different, fun ways.

Glossary

fixed mindset — If you are using a fixed mindset, you believe that your intelligence is fixed and can't be changed

growth mindset — If you are using a growth mindset, you believe that your intelligence is always changing because your brain can grow stronger

neurons — Cells in your brain that pass information back and forth to each other

persevere — To keep going even when things get difficult

resilience — The ability to stay positive and make an effort even when things are challenging, and to recover quickly from difficulties

unconscious — Not aware of something

Index

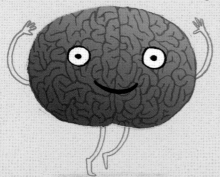

Notes for adults

The concept of a "growth mindset" was developed by psychologist Carol Dweck, and is used to describe a way in which effective learners view themselves as being on a constant journey to develop their intelligence. This is supported by studies showing how our brains continue to develop throughout our lives, rather than intelligence and ability being static.

Responding with a growth mindset means being eager to learn more and seeing that making mistakes and getting feedback about how to improve are important parts of that journey.

A growth mindset is at one end of a continuum, and learners move between this and a "fixed mindset"—which is based on the belief that you're either smart or you're not.

A fixed mindset is unhelpful because it can make learners feel they need to "prove" rather than develop their intelligence. They may avoid challenges, not wanting to risk failing at anything, and this reluctance to make mistakes—and learn from them—can negatively affect the learning process.

Help children develop a growth mindset by:

- Giving specific positive feedback on their learning efforts, such as "Well done, you've been practicing..." rather than non-specific praise, such as "Good effort" or comments such as "Smart girl/boy!" that can encourage fixed-mindset thinking.

- Sharing times when you have had to persevere with learning something new and what helped you succeed.

- Encouraging them to keep a learning journal, where they can explore what they learn from new challenges and experiences.

- Making sure they understand that being resilient doesn't mean they're not allowed to feel worried or sad, it's just a way of helping them to recover and keep going.